ECLIPSE SEASON

POEMS BY

Karin **GOTTSHALL**

CONDUIT
BOOKS & EPHEMERA

ECLIPSE SEASON

FOR LIZA—

Printed in the United States of America

ISBN: 979-8-9883272-8-8

Published by Conduit Books & Ephemera
788 Osceola Avenue
Saint Paul, Minnesota 55105
www.conduit.org

Book design by Scott Bruno/b graphic design

Distributed by Itasca Books
www.itascabooks.com

Cover image: Total solar eclipse, courtesy NASA/Keegan Barber; William Strode, *Collecting Rocks and Shells Along the Banks of the Ohio River, June 1972*, courtesy U.S. National Archives; additional images Shutterstock.

CONTENTS

II.

ECLIPSE SEASON

Origin Story

Lake Michigan dreamed me, I think,
in the winter of 1969, its long currents
combing shipwrecks and where

was my mama, then? (She was wearing
a red muumuu.) And where was my father,
then? (He was fishing for steelhead.)

No one dreamed you, stupid girl, the seagull
said—*you came straight from the belly*
of your granddad's school mascot.

You wore plaid skirts and bruised your knees
and lived across the street from the motorcycle shop.
I remember dropping dimes in the jukebox,

I remember embers in the sand. Once I saw God
himself—a small boy running across the RV park
with a toy sword in his hand. I dreamed

we all lay down on the beach and the dunes
moved over our bodies. It took
ten thousand years of whispering,

but we finally slept. *And before that?*
the seagull asked. Before that I found comfort
in the fur of animals and the movement

of a boat on the water. I was warm
in my mother's arms. Before that I was
a sonic boom over Wisconsin, and before that, fire.

I.

The Last Ice Age

I have a habit of withdrawing
into the Pleistocene epoch

I empty all my language into the fire
and my skull grows large with silence

At night I fall into the sky

I take a dog to bed
and sleep until we both need meat

The stars tell me nothing
I do not need to know

Everyone I've ever loved has been keen with hunger

Everyone I've lost has been buried
with their bone beads
and there is no need to visit their graves

I am on the wide plain with the running horses

My body is a simple instrument for the wind to play

We go around mistaking the wind

for people we know. Through the walls,
it sounds like the girls in my dormitory
twenty years ago. Weeping when they thought
everyone was asleep. We mistake the world's memory
for our own, though we will never be that old.
We go around with our maps, our calculators,
our little clocks. But this morning when you left
without your umbrella, I ran outside
to put my arms around you. We think the rain
remembers us. And your déjà vu, you must
have dreamed it—or had we been there
before? Weather impartial, unsettled
above and filtering through our thin jackets,
our skins. My mistake to hold you back
just when you'd nearly found our borders,
to intrude upon your memory of holding a woman
who was really only the rain.

The Human League

Nights I can't sleep I remember the rotary
phone—long for it deep in the finger joints

and wrists. In high school I had such insomnia.
Have you ever forgotten how to have a body,

even as the body you have violently resists
its own irrelevance? All I could think to do

was listen to the radio: the hits
and the butterscotch voice of the overnight DJ.

The lines were always wide open when I called,
and before long I understood he was just as lonely

and almost as tired as I was. Who knows
what happens to those weird connections

made when longing and technology
commute our sludgy bodies into pure energy,

flung recklessly and in search of a place to land?
We had so much to talk about, there in the blue light

of our receivers and controls, the volume needle's
loose play across the dial's face—my first

and most glorious nothing. We never
met, which made it more intimate—

just the closeness of a voice heard
through headphones. A conversation interrupted

every time a record ended. It was always
a song about someone just wishing for release.

The Origins of Desire

I think I want summer—round
        and blue as girlhood. It comes
with smoke. Music drifting soft
        from the valley as boreal forests
burn. I still listen for the owl—
        a heavy nightdress. Rubber boots.
When I was small—an egg
        in a delicate eggcup. The weather
today begins as mist, barely falling.
        On my smallest screen I watch
an entire home lifted by a river
        and hurled downstream.

Tell My Fortune

Ask the glowing screen. Ask the dog
with her bloody feet, running across Alabama.

Ask the ghost, body buried under the pantry.
We all have to be no one to someone.

You are out there, somewhere in a place I have
never slept: on a boat, or a bed too small,

under a water-stained ceiling. How can I
be no one, wearing these soft skin boots

over my own soft skin? The sun goes down, earth
churns its heaviest stones. Curve

of shoulder, the old tattoo. Unmet, I am still
no one to you. And I know myself too well.

Sycamore Street

All that winter the wind
Bashed the borders of my district.

The birds and other animals
Had taken their hunger,

Their feathers and soft coats.
Every morning my uniform

Was starched and waiting
And I yawned on the city bus as we idled

At the red light beside the cemetery gate.
Poor Patience Post, I thought, buried

Like a nut. Buds tender
In her silken ears, two seats up,

A young nurse applied mascara.
Cold air scented by paper cups

Of steamed oat milk; each passenger
With her difficult, unspoken questions.

The wind troubled the trees at the edge
Of the county. Poor Ellen, wife

Of Arthur. Her desire. And
Her song a mouthful of stone.

After you left

the bears arrived,
pushing over
the compost bin,
tipping the garbage
to leave a stinking
trail of onion skins
and oil—everything
I had disposed of
and never wanted
to see again—that led
from the can
and into the woods.
I hated you
even more for going
then, as each
morning I cleaned
the evidence of hunger
and destruction
from the driveway—
the filth of my life
without you—this life
you'd entered and trashed
before lumbering back
into the wilderness
you came from.

A Poverty

Through childhood I was shadowed
by the bluish sound of my mother's sigh.

Many hours in my room alone
with a toy space ship—

but I was happiest in the basement,
where the fire lived and the cats

hid from the landlord when he dropped by.
I practiced saying "sea-faring, spindrift,

Antikythera." Words fluent
and articulated as wood lice. And

my baby teeth for a handful
of change. The wind is no one's meal.

49th Parallel

It must be cold
On the ridge where you sing
You are telling your life
Not to me
I listen through my dreams
Something hungry in the snow
Under stars
I am not a beautiful animal
Where can I put my desire?
In the quarry
Far from your den
Your cry fits exactly
The contours of my room
You have been telling
I called it singing
Something I needed
But it is not for me

Pasture

Today I drive into the country, passing fields
of sheep and small houses made of stone.
To live inside stone—I always want to be
headed someplace like that, unshakable.
As for you—nothing about you ever suggested
any kind of arrival. Not your words or soft hands.
And your death, a departure that pulled
every bird and pasture back through its opening.
If it were summer I would swim underwater,
floating between sky and the pond's pebbled floor.
My body has become itself only in relation
to your absence, the continuation of it all these years,
what you never saw coming. You were right there.
No, you were somewhere out in the weather and I was still
in that other, shimmering field. Holding my breath.

Because I never mastered

being a daughter, I failed
to become someone's mother.
And whose daughter am I
now? Even the grass
won't claim me, even
the clouds. I practice motherhood
on dogs and berry vines.
Tell me again how much
I am missing—a child to grasp
my fingers in her tight fist.
Was I that kind of daughter,
once? Or was I born with my
hands this open, with this face
that could be anyone's?

Fugue

Someone hung a bell in a tree,
and the tree grew and the bell

still rings high above the street
when the wind is up—up

where the wind doesn't know
a single human soul,

and the tree doesn't know
it isn't a boat, and the street

is a long long river; once
I knew I was a woman alone

in a bed among trees—
but since then the bell

has forgotten who hung it,
has emptied itself of everything

but the wind, and forgotten finally
the tree, and why it still rings.

Ghosted

Have you noticed, Love,
how over days the quality of the silence

between us has changed? Dead air becoming
a dry streambed, a state bird of quiet;

static humming down to heartbeat. If we
keep it up we will compile an ocean of it,

wave on wave of silence, of knowing
no one will speak or has spoken, but still

communicating something that touches the time
when we were. This silence asks from us

only the most tender attention
to its deepening. No one needs to respond.

The Softer Side of Sears

If there is one thing you've learned
from a half-century of living
with appliances, it's that they keep their own
counsel. And that humming heals. Consider
the basement dehumidifier, slowly
pulling your tears from the air.
It could say something about mercy,
but instead it simply fills its little bucket.
Consider the microwave: its tiny light
comes on reliably. The refrigerator's souvenir
magnets fastened to photos of your dog
comprise the closest thing you have to a shrine.
The washer and dryer are sex-obsessed,
down there rocking. They know everything
about you and your loneliness—
they could say something regarding
desire and the impossible desert of a Tuesday
evening. Instead they're just swishing
the soapy water, pleasuring themselves
in these final, reckless days of their warranties.

Answers for the Algorithm

The loneliest I've ever been
was in bed with my ex,

imagining how many boxes
it would take to pack all my books.

The best sex I've ever had
was with a man who told me

he loved me, and married
someone else a week later.

In my fantasies, every shame
is redeemed and the pain

feels like desire, is held
by someone stronger

than I've ever actually met.
Here are the photos of a time

I forgot for a moment I was burning.
The most private thing I'll admit

is that I know exactly
what I'm looking for.

From the Testimony of Vulnerable and Endangered Moths

I was once believed extinct—
I knew better, but my unborn daughters
will never inherit my box of silver rings.

I'm a one-year species, like a minor grieving.
Listen, I am not trying to be beautiful, I am
just trying to live. Born of a cream-colored egg

on salt grass, scattered over grasslands—
Mother burned in a brush fire while I danced,
a teenager with my hem unstitched,

and the closest I came to beauty
was the new shade of lipstick I stole
from the pharmacy. The names

of my scars are Thorn, Thunder,
Theory of Nectar. Because the taste of this world
tasted like my own self, I thought I could stay.

Because to live by superstition means to reside always
in the county of Disaster—my best hope
is a horseshoe or a buried tooth.

I am federally listed as endangered, born out
of the sky, diurnal, to drink from purple vetch
and Canada thistle. I am loose-shaken

upon prairies, right-of-ways, live
in a tent of two leaves silked together.
No, not beautiful—but I am crafty

and feral. Have many eyes. Goodbye to my feet,
those organs of taste. I easily interpret the dream
the world never had of me; and the dream it has

of my body spread and pinned to a board.
When I'm gone I'll be the ghost of strong hands
lifting a child. The ghost of nascent things.

Ghost of a woman standing in the shower
while the water runs—washing the salt
from her face, the dust from her wings.

My tall grown son walks wordless

past me in a dark field, where crickets
chirr and the wind carries
a smell of burning wood.
He wears a Spanish wedding gown:
stiff black lace over whalebone
cinched tight. Hem scraping
the dry scrub of the field. I watch him
move toward a white ladder
that rises higher than I can see.
I think I could still follow him—
and realize that is something
I have always believed, even though
I can't remember my son's name,
or what it was to give birth to him.
I watch his still face behind the veil,
the pale skin of his hands. I should
go to him, and offer the lemons
from my palms. I should offer to climb
the ladder instead. My strong son,
this bride, so grave as he climbs
slowly higher, until his black gown
vanishes against unbroken black above.

Horseshoe Bay

Was I really born
of my own bold mother—
all ferocity and diving
underwater? I stood shivering
on the dock while she crossed
the lake. I watched her strong,
tan arms. And four decades passed
before she remembered to return,
no—she was back by sunset and then
put her mind to other things.

I put my own mind to nights
of childhood so dark my body
threatened to dissolve into deepest sleep.
The damp thumbprint of the summer
solstice. I've always been old—
it's a trick I learned to keep
from aging. How could I trust
such depths and currents? From where
I stood she seemed to slip,
in all her youth and energy,
below the horizon's curve.
If I had a hundred daughters
to swim away from, I still
would never be that young.

The Stones

Walked an hour or so along the railroad tracks.
Chicory and Queen Anne's lace. Buzzing sun.

Came home with a tick on my knee. Who decided
on the sound of the dial tone? When

was the last time I heard it? Time isn't
spent like pennies—it is the fountain

the pennies are thrown into. The neighbor's
motion-detector goes off when the fox

walks across the lawn. Last thing I remembered
before I died was dropping a needle

with a hiss onto the spinning black disc
of my mother's favorite Stones album.

Desire

I want the dark inside the vessel.
The hollow of a bone flute. I want

fire ticking at the iron, weight
of a belt at the hips. This cupboard I am

kept in is fetid with the smell of moth eggs. I want
to pull my undoing backwards through my body,

darning my organs whole. I want the light
behind the beloved, to lick rust

from the hinges. I want sandals
on the path warm with rosemary. In all the world's

excess of time, horror to feel it
narrowing to nothing—gone the movement

of water on the river in the wake of a girl's
crossing, and even the poverty

of waiting in the rain, just outside the door.

Passion

Who says there is no soul in the design
of modern urban hotels. Cities

in Canada are all so clean, you said—
it was not praise. You were holding

my hand, which might have felt
like intimacy. The season that had been

my favorite no longer excited me.
Lights over the reservoir reassured us.

I was reminded of the weather radar—
wanting to be outside myself—all that disturbed

air and distance. My mother had finished
her course of radiation. I thought,

how many more nights like this
are allotted me. It felt like need.

Even driving to meet you, I experienced
a kind of rage. The wide green fields.

Solstice

Winter turns my brothers
into noisy crows.

I'm drinking wine all night
with the ghost of our mother

while they roost
in the big pines.

One brother dies
for every hour of darkness,

and I was never told
the spell to release them.

Even if I knew, my body
is a series of locks rusted

shut, whose workings words
cannot move through.

December is a poltergeist,

noisy with carols and nor'easters. My family
is a wolf pack, and we celebrate Christmas
stalking something timid and gamey: a good

night's sleep or lost souvenir spoon
from a trip to Montréal.
Lo, the churchyard bears the symbol

of a virgin birth: a nativity whose sheep
keep turning up on the ridge, throats
slit. I light a candle in the cathedral, try to find a place

where the urge to scream is less consuming.
It's a nuisance-haunting, and I try to hide it.
I hunt for a spirit-box or carol—*hallelujah!*—

with something to tell me other than
childless one, shivering blood-thing on the snow,
your mama is dead and your house is so cold.

The daughters you didn't have

are doing fine without you—
they're playing house in the particle
accelerator. The children
by the deli meat case have smeared
the glass with sticky handprints
and you remember how,
heartbroken at twenty,
you woke up in a tent
outside of London—buttery dawn
through ripstop nylon, crying
babies, little lambs in the thicket.

Survivalism

When I'm gone you can toss my ashes
into Lake Champlain or misplace them

among the boxes in the shed, whatever.
I am daughter only to a working dog,

a shepherd with one blind eye and an ethic.
He remembers he loves me each morning

and howls when I leave for work.
When my mother died I found the things

she'd collected for the apocalypse:
canned beans and bandages. She was ready,

I guess, but it made me sad to think
of her living there alone—the whole world

having undreamt itself utterly,
the horizon in flames—wondering

what day it was, and whether I'd survived.

A Common Occurrence

My mother died on her birthday,
in a white room in the hospital's old wing,
when I stepped out for coffee. Ten minutes,
tops—though I'd been there for days, listening
to her breathe. The nurses said that happens
more than you'd think. Once the life
support is removed, the family sits
at the bedside a week, sometimes,
and then the person dies
while everyone's out for a smoke.
I was given one hour with her body. The brain
cannot make sense of a person converted
to object. I kept seeing her move.
It seemed important, so I told
the aids who finally came in to clean her
that it was her birthday. I said
I knew she was dead, but I kept
seeing her breathe, and I laughed a little,
because it seemed crazy, but maybe
it meant something. And they said yes,
that happens all the time.

Theft

In the second year of my sojourn
on this earth I went under

the knife. Some soft part I'd never
seen. Rose up from sleep

as through the weight of pressing
galaxies, and where the part had been

felt only the blackness of before-birth,
felt the place the blade had sheared,

felt emptiness as a form
of my erasure. For a long time

I tasted nothing but vowels.
When the stuffed owl's eye came off

and I stepped on it barefoot,
I wouldn't walk for a week. Held my own

eyes shut so they wouldn't fall out.
When next I saw him—sutures

to remove—I bit the surgeon's
big white hand. Sound

of animals crying through their open
mouths. I've held my body so tightly

to myself, I hold it so quietly:
all my floating organs clenched

beneath locked bones I know
were never mine to keep.

Inheritance

Her books, her plants, her ancient cat.
Her dream journals, her sweet tooth, her Versa.

Her childhood tap shoes. Expired meds.
Four hundred dollars in dimes.

An antique christening bonnet,
a walker she never had the chance to use.

Her cherry bed, her paintings. Her chicken bones
stashed in a basket by the back door.

Her insomnia, her sewing machine. A shed
full of saws. Her ashes, her guitar.

Her Ritalin. One hundred and seventeen pads
of Post-It notes. A closet full of broken lamps.

Her corkscrews, her boots, (too big), her drapes,
her dresser, her kettles, her board games.

The ring she wore to the hospital
and gave me one day when she could still talk,

Take this. It's nice but I won't need it anymore.

Symbolic Gestures

So you've emptied into the mystery.
The wind knots reeds and thickets.

When I say the word *wind* I'm saying I believe
in an afterlife without the burden

of consciousness, and it's a relief
to see you released. Ashes

on the sweetness of the lake. With you
died some of my tangled selves. It's a relief—

familiar as the scent of stone—to drop
myself again into the well of grief.

II.

Poem with Lines from My Mother's Dream Journal

1.

I was swept a very long distance—
the churchyards along Route 22 filling with snow.
I arrived to find you blank with pain.

The road I had come on was flooded:
sometimes you couldn't even remember which organ was removed,
what remained.

Eighteen hours in the ER
and you told my grandmother through the phone,
Give my soul to beauty.

A body floating alone.

You sang in your gown,
you thought you were home, the orange cat walking across the blanket.
I heard the triage nurse questioning a patient in the hallway:

> Why did you set yourself on fire?
> Have you ever set yourself on fire before?
> What were you thinking when you set yourself on fire?

This I feel to be the work of God, so I submit—

I was thinking I was small and dirty once,
and my mother washed my face.

2.

The seasons of the world were changing.

Weed above, roots below.

I could hear you as soon as I entered the unit,

There's someone else in this boat.

Morphine made you a traveler, when it didn't make you sad.

I almost went home last night.

Ninety degrees, no wind. The precision of helicopters
landing on the roof as you drifted.

I stood outside your room when they changed the dressing
so I wouldn't have to see the scars again.

I recognized her then, a woman pouring spirit into matter.

You said you saw them, so many, above you, on the ceiling.

Later I dreamed I found you walking alone on the railroad tracks.

Come home, you're sick.

The seasons were changing.

I left the hospital in the dark, driving over the Hudson River,

This is my country now.

I let myself into your empty house with a new-cut key—

The weird clicking, grinding sound of my heart.

3.

I flew past a tree that was hung with little cloth dolls—

Near the border there was always that same darkness, the smell of river water.

The ICU doctor told me it was my decision.

I followed the dried stroke of a paintbrush up to the ceiling—

He said he had been there before. Believed we come back.

When next I am your daughter I will remind you of that.

They cleared the room to remove the breathing tube.

I remembered at the border, a darkness. My purse on the passenger seat.

You never woke up again, except to cry out when the nurses turned you.

Once I slept in your living room, the weight of the train
softly ringing the strings of your guitar,

but now I sleep with my head on your hospital bed
while the sky turns green before the rain.

This intimacy with your life, your death—I never asked for.

We were going through a valley and were sad to leave it.

The sound was of loud water, and not humming.

I remembered at the border, a darkness. Something
I had carried there with me.

4.

I had just wanted to see the ocean,
but you gave me a heavy bowl of water
that reflected the constellation Cassiopeia.
You asked me to carry it until it evaporated
or turned to ice.

This is not my fight,
In your garden I pulled up root vegetables
but they were too woody to eat,
misshapen from growing between stones.

Now your house hoards its electricity
like a held breath. When I step
into the estuary I feel the sockets
of my bones, flayed clean.
The beginnings of the dream are lost.

Language left me and I lost

my voice screaming on the ridge.
Seasons came I had

no name for. Gesture
by gesture I fell

into every sort of disrepair,
stashing the ashes of those I'd loved

in the attic instead
of scattering them toward beauty

as they'd asked. Out of loneliness,
yes—but they never spoke.

In my silence I soured
like milk, long-wintered

on rage. The ridge creatured
me, roots cutting my feet

while the objects of the house
loomed motionless,

listening, like ancestors gathered
to hear my prayers for them—

my mouth an unspent purse
for the dead to covet—

but I had only ugly sounds
and an uglier, wordless grief.

Evensong

Tonight all up against my own failings,
and tomorrow's just another Tuesday.

I have one shoelace that will never
stay tied; I have a bagful of music. Lord, I have

no brother. The rabbit of morning snags
her tooth on me. I guess Adam was a luthier

and Eve a rhododendron. Do you ever sing
your own vespers? What's to become of my small

fingerbones, the tiny bones of my ears? Thanks be
to God for keeping me down. Panting.

Thanks for passing around the paper collection plate
on which I place the single violet of my breath.

My sleep lives in the house

with the broken stoop
with the phone forever
off the hook. My sleep lives
under three quilts
in the room where the dog
stretches and breathes
in the room where time
has stopped its turn and night
is an arc of stars
across the window's gap. My sleep
lives in the space between
grief and calendar
between watch and water glass.
My sleep lives in the stillness
of a house bound by winter
of a life I keep forgetting
the substance of
between the looping choir
of a month of moons and the dawn
of the cold day my sleep
survives and until I die it pulls
me dreaming heavy down.

To My Ancestors

I'm your girl, as quiet as you were, as hungry—
a lifetime of eating off your chipped stoneware.

My hair turns white at the temples;
my father opens another steamer trunk

full of your embroidered gowns.
A tiny box to hold the bones

of your house pet. And you're in the very
soot of the place. Your girl is up late,

just as you were, wondering what it's like
to pack the house and move into the dirt.

All these evenings, so much to do, my fingers
bleeding. This is America, where storms

swing like glass chandeliers over the Atlantic.
You passed down your recipes

and your sturdy walnut bed, a deck of cards,
your prophesies, and the gesture meaning *goodbye*—

did it pain you, to leave them behind?
Such practical things, that bear repeated use.

Rites

Soft white moon of a blister, burst
on my heel from yesterday's sandal.

The bell in the tree.

Once, for removal of a tumor in my uterus
I traded two hours of myself: out cold
on the table.

Sound of the wind when you live
on the plains.

Her thumbprint published at the lip
of the fired pot she made
before I was born:

my mother is just a piece of blue
floating through the house.

Tame

The feral cat I've tethered since September
to a supply of Fancy Feast still has all her distrust intact—
she keeps her distance, even on the coldest nights.
I am still not quite familiar with myself, either, I guess.
I get lost in the cemetery, looking for my ancestors, tripping on roots.
What I've always liked about my family
is the way no one ever says how they really feel,
so it is possible to imagine anything.
I make sure to tell the cat *I love you,*
so she will not have to become a poet, like me.
She moves like a girl who has never been burdened
with her own reflection. I remember that I used to like my shoulders,
and growing up it seemed that boys liked them too—
but it has been a long time since I gave them much thought.
It's a shame when the particulars of yourself start to disappear
into the routine of days you didn't make
and have little stake in. These days I tell my students
the point of discomfort is interesting to investigate—
but I know that I am usually not that brave.
I'm a housecat, really. I swore off heartbreak
after the last one carved me up in the standard way.
I told myself I'll die if I'm not tamed.
I say *Kitty, this is your bowl. Your very own.*
Behind the house the weeds are full of Greek mythology,
and the last full moon kept me up for two nights straight.
But the frost is coming. I creep closer and closer
to the woodstove. Soon I will be all the way inside,
docile to the point that anyone might put a match to me
and be warmed by my burning for a long, long time.

Vireo

The house of the dead
film director was in my dreams

all night. Again. Mid-century,
concrete, I was in a dream

in his movie in my dream.
This morning the china cup

feels too fragile. I feel too fragile:
bone china, language dripping

from my skull to coat my spine.
Syllables splash against city

streets and traffic as my mind
drifts elsewhere—through the syrup.

An app on my phone helps me
identify the songs of birds. Her song

illuminates in gold script
the shadowed parking structure.

Ash

The river has its own concerns. It loves
the human form the way fury

loves a stone. In the shed, I stacked
the objects of my mother's desire

in labeled boxes. The juddering water,
the urn. After I'd done her final taxes

I felt it: she was burned to ash. Fury
loves a stone the way a house is haunted,

the way a house can love you, just
walking through. A chipped bowl,

a broken tooth. Her shoes kicked off
at the bottom of the stairs.

Marriage

He learns to say no by saying
nothing. She doesn't mind
another trip up the stairs.

When they've both left for work
the sofa can finally let out its belt
and breathe. Later, he spreads

oil in a pan; she thinks
If I mow the lawn he will never
leave. The wrecks

of their childhoods are burnt
ruins at the bottom
of the toaster.

Their rolled-up tent smells
like old rain and menstruation.
At night the sofa dreams

of a journey by train.
He has been standing in this stream
so long it's all he remembers.

She resists the urge to climb
into the kitchen cupboard,
holding her ears.

I disappoint the stars

with my weeping, and the moon
with my barrenness. I let down

the wind when I love
the dirt road and the hatchet

more than my home, my wedding
band. Disappoint time

with my hurried breath
and heartbeat, the earth

with my weight. Even the shadows
have turned away—gray ghosts

of everything I cannot
keep, and cannot appease.

The Blue Horse

I want to go out in the rain
and look for the blue horse
from my sister's dream.
It's Tuesday night and I should be sleeping,

but I want to go out in the rain
and talk to the compost bins
because I feel smaller than the tiny line,
the symbol for *minus*. If I found the blue horse,

maybe it would carry me to the simple room
where my sister has been all these years
with her violin and her thick math books.
The music that comes from her windows

sounds like the song the creek sings
when it thinks no one is listening—
but it's only the sound of equations
solving themselves and the wind at play

within the body of the violin. I know
the horse is alone, somewhere,
in the darkness of its field, rain falling
on its flanks. I want to go to it, and all

that holds me back is the same shyness
that marks my inability to pray. The night
is deepening around it. I recognize
those shadows. My sister dreamed this,

and because she was never born
everything my sister dreams is true.

The Twelfth Century

I left myself asleep in a hotel room in Montréal,
a spacecraft bound for the edge of the galaxy.

Grainy film with burnt-out frames: the taste
of the monkey bars in third grade.

A feeling that everything good was denied you, except
what you were able to hold so quietly it was almost a form of theft.

The house across the street is all lit up at midnight:
a shipping container, the raw material of plastic dolls.
Laws of dress. Laws of acceptable speech.
How many eyelashes awash in the ocean?

Climbing into a cabinet to rest, climbing into
the twelfth century, between convent walls.

The river is a girl playing solitaire—
blue ink on her sleeve.

The Waiting Room

The moon floats across the window
like a patient in a paper gown.

She feels time move through her ghost.

Under fluorescent lights, a thriving tree with heart-shaped leaves.

Names are spoken at the threshold.

She feels pain's shape, fluid in space.

The animal grief rises up,
but in the chair with chevron upholstery
she maintains an almost human face.

She watches another woman's child play with a blue alligator.

Shame pools in her organs while music no one wrote
is piped in from nowhere.

Orbit

My first love was a little green boat.
In my kitchen I Google satellite images
of the lake. I think I see myself, bandy
and suntanned, rowing into the dip
of the bay. But that was years before
this satellite was forged, in a decade
during which men had somehow travelled
to the moon. There was always sand
between my toes; at night I shook it loose
from my ears. All these years I've imagined
the green boat floating alone on that big lake
waiting for me the way my sweet dog
waits outside every door I'm closed behind.
I got older but still believed
my interrupted games could be picked up again,
someday, like the smooth stones I collected
along the sandspit. In my green boat, my swimsuit
with poodles on it—no one warns us
that what we've chosen to love can never
be put away. I thought it was safe
to push off into that sky-reflecting lake.

Camera Obscura

The neighbors called the cops on Mom and me
the night we broke into our own apartment—
not as dramatic as it sounds. We'd left
the kitchen window open a crack and I was seven

and skinny enough to shimmy through. I hadn't thought
of it in years, but last night I dreamt of that neighborhood,
our building—it had become a prison
for the dead, a heavy gate preventing entrance,

and I spoke to my mother through the iron bars.
When I see her like that she never mentions
her death or the time that's passed, but I
have the feeling she'd rather not be bothered. If dream-

people are aspects of ourselves given voice then who
inside me is she? She's so angry. Or if
she is my mother and I am granted
these visitations, then I think she'd prefer I just

move on. When I remember my childhood bedroom
I think of the ceiling, on which through some small gap
on sunny days I saw projected a bird's eye image
of the parking lot behind the building.

Lying on my bed I watched as her gray car
pulled into its space. A spirit floating
above the blacktop, I saw her bend
to pet the neighbors' cat before she dug

in her purse for a cigarette. How long have I been
haunting her? That night the reds and blues
bounced off the eggshell walls and the officers
had to write a report even though

the neighbors came over and helped
clear everything up. We all had a good laugh.
She didn't tell them we'd been at the bar—
an omission so weightless it floated—

but anyway I liked the bar, I liked the walk there
and the walk home, holding her hand. I liked that I fit
through the narrow opening of the window
and the feeling when I touched down

and set my palms on the cold tile floor.
I liked that moment alone in the darkness,
the kitchen's strange inversion, as I decided
whether or not to unbolt the door and let her in.

Claim

I spent most of fourth grade in outer space.
Those red pants with the slight flare.

This restlessness—obviously not new. Ruined
with everything translucent.

One fevered day in bed, another, another.
My mother in the kitchen, cooking a fish.

When I light a cigarette our bus will come,
she always said, and it did. Ground under her heel.

Lemon-scented soap, pine sap, roses.
A jump-rope truth I can no longer access.

In dreams my mother is without substance,
without dimension. Without love—an empty boat.

Day like a heavy black kettle.
The half-asleep feeling, I could go back and claim it.

A cup of coffee forgotten on the windowsill:
a conjugation of the verb "to haunt."

My House Is My Mother Now

Her cupboards are filled with bowls.
I lean into her when the hail
comes, I tell her all my
mistakes. My house hums
to me, and shuts the closet
full of dresses, the drawer
of yellowed teeth. My house
is my mother now: she dreams
of burning while I sleep.

Atlantis

The flood enters the house
in the night, a cunning

intruder, rising to leave
its wet frescoes darkening

above baseboards,
rendering the bed

stranded, up to its ankles,
while you dream

you are a girl again—
entering the water cautiously

on thin, unsteady legs
to cast your tiny toy net.

Eclipse Season

Clouds darken and spoil over the hills
Then crabapple petals come down with the rain

In the house where the glassblower lived
In the field behind the radio tower

Horseshoes and ashes

I once stood at the curve of that road
Eyes adjusting to darkness to witness the comet

A controlled burn

When she was dying a guitar kept her warm
Time is music expressed through human bones

Midlife

I am a hickory wand turned
white cow, slow and lowing.

The river is tuned to the key
of thunder—at night I hear it

rolling over its heaviest stones.
I've learned a game

to play with desire: hide and
hide again. I'm still

in the cupboard, holding
my breath. The owl

catches one more shrew
and the basements on my street

slowly fill with water, as they have
for a million years, at least.

Geminids

I lost myself drunk
on the porch, watching

the meteors,
and vertigo turned me

upside down—strings of light
tied to my wrists.

Then loose-harnessed
in no one's arms—

the skull an interpreter
of pleasures, suddenly

weightless. In my soft,
ongoing body I have

to bear it—starlight
a poverty to my eyes—

this dark sky I've dropped
myself back through.

The Lake

I row my small boat
through shallows.
The universe ends
where fog begins
on the rocky bank—
nothing exists
except one crow
rattling above
the outcrop. In all
my time on earth
I have learned one
word. My mouth
holds it like a coin.
Almost soundless,
water ripples
where my oar dips,
pulling the scent
of copper from the lake.
Eddies open in the wake,
all I cannot say—
my arms pulse
with the weight of it.

ACKNOWLEDGMENTS

Love and thanks to my poetry sisters Alison Prine and Spring Ulmer, who offered so much generous feedback, wisdom, and support as this book was being written and assembled.

Gratitude to my dad, to family near and far and in the hereafter, to my students and colleagues at Middlebury College, and to my teachers and friends from birth to the present.

To William Waltz and everyone at Conduit, thank you for the honor of selecting *Eclipse Season* for your catalog—I'm so proud to be included—and for all you do in support of literature.

I also extend thanks to the readers and editors of the following journals, where versions of some of these poems were first published:

Bellevue Literary Review: "Ash," "Fugue," and "Evensong"

The Colorado Review: "We go around mistaking the wind"

Diode: "The Softer Side of Sears" and "Inheritance"

FIELD: "Poem with Lines from My Mother's Dream Journal"

Four Way Review: "December is a Poltergeist" and "The Last Ice Age"

The Gettysburg Review: "Desire" and "The Human League"

Juked: "Survivalism"

The Kenyon Review: "Origin Story"

Pratik: "From the Testimony of Vulnerable and Endangered Moths"

Raleigh Review: "Passion," "Pasture," and "The Twelfth Century"

Red Rock Review: "Tame"

ABOUT THE AUTHOR

Karin Gottshall is the author of two previous award-winning poetry books: *Crocus* (Fordham University Press) and *The River Won't Hold You* (Ohio State University Press). She has also published three limited-edition chapbooks with Argos Books and Dancing Girl Press. Gottshall's poems have appeared in *The Kenyon Review, The Colorado Review, diode,* and many other publications. She lives in Vermont and teaches creative writing at Middlebury College.

OTHER TITLES FROM CONDUIT BOOKS & EPHEMERA

Where is Everyone! by Elizabeth Zuba

Ghost in the Archive by Jennifer Loyd

Bright Life, Animal Heart by Laura Minor

Beneath All Water by Zackary Medlin

Extremely Expensive Mystical Experiences for Astronauts by Dara Barrois/Dixon

Autoblivion by Trey Moody

The Art of Bagging by Joshua Gottlieb-Miller

Thunderbird Inn by Collin Callahan

The Birthday of the Dead by Rachel Abramowitz

The World to Come by David Keplinger

Present Tense Complex by Suphil Lee Park

Sacrificial Metal by Esther Lee

The Miraculous, Sometimes by Meg Shevenock

The Last Note Becomes Its Listener by Jeffrey Morgan

Animul/Flame by Michelle Lewis